Crafting Your Perfect LLC

From Concept to Creation

Daichi A. Kenzo

Copyright © 2024 by Daichi A. Kenzo

All rights reserved.

No part of this publication may be reproduced, distributed, or transmitted in any form or by any means, including photocopying, recording, or other electronic or mechanical methods, without the prior written permission of the publisher, except in the case of brief quotations embodied in critical reviews and certain other noncommercial uses permitted by copyright law.

Published by Daichi A. Kenzo

Preface

Welcome to Crafting Your Perfect LLC: From Concept to Creation. This book is designed to be your comprehensive guide to understanding and establishing your Limited Liability Company (LLC) in simple, easy-to-follow language.

Starting a business can be daunting, especially when it comes to navigating the legal intricacies of forming an LLC. Whether you're a budding entrepreneur or a seasoned business owner looking to expand, this book is here to demystify the process and empower you to make informed decisions every step of the way.

In the following chapters, we'll explore the foundational concepts of LLCs, from understanding what an LLC is and why it might be the right choice for your business, to the practical steps involved in its formation. Along the journey, we'll cover important topics such as choosing the right business structure, drafting an effective operating agreement, and complying with state regulations.

But this book is more than just a how-to guide. It's a roadmap tailored to your entrepreneurial journey, filled with real-world examples, expert tips, and practical insights to help you craft an LLC that not only meets your business needs but also sets you up for long-term success.

Whether you're dreaming of launching the next big tech startup or simply looking to turn your passion project into a profitable venture, Crafting Your Perfect LLC is your indispensable companion on the path to entrepreneurial success.

Daichi A. Kenzo

2024

Table of Contents

Introduction
Understanding the Concept of Limited Liability Companies.
Why Choose an LLC Structure?
Overview of What's Covered.

Chapter 1: Setting the Foundation
1.1 Evaluating Your Business Idea.
1.2 Assessing Feasibility and Viability.
1.3 Defining Your Mission and Vision.

Chapter 2: Legal Framework
2.1 The Basics of Business Law and Regulations.
2.2 Comparing Business Structures: LLCs vs. Other Entities.
2.3 Understanding Legal Liabilities and Protections.

Chapter 3: Forming Your LLC
3.1 Step-by-Step Guide to LLC Formation.
3.2 Choosing the Right State for Registration.
3.3 Naming Your LLC: Tips and Considerations.

Chapter 4: Crafting Your Operating Agreement.
4.1 Importance and Components of an Operating Agreement.
4.2 Customizing Your Agreement to Fit Your Business Needs.
4.3 Common Mistakes to Avoid.

Chapter 5: Tax Matters
5.1 Tax Implications of LLCs.
5.2 Understanding Pass-through Taxation.
5.3 Strategies for Tax Optimization.

Chapter 6: Managing Your LLC
6.1 Roles and Responsibilities of LLC Members.
6.2 Effective Communication and Decision-Making.
6.3 Handling Disputes and Challenges.

Chapter 7: Growing Your LLC
7.1 Scaling Strategies and Expansion Plans.
7.2 Funding Options for LLC Growth.
7.3 Building a Strong Brand and Reputation.

Chapter 8: Compliance and Maintenance
8.1 Annual Requirements and Ongoing Obligations.

8.2 Staying Compliant with State and Federal Regulations.
8.3 Strategies for Long-Term Success.

Conclusion.
Recap of Key Points.
Final Thoughts and Next Steps.

Introduction

This book, "Crafting Your Perfect LLC," is a comprehensive guide created to bring clarity around Limited Liability Companies (LLCs) and leave you empowered with knowledge so that you can make better decisions about your business structure. Whether you are just starting out as an entrepreneur or an expert in business ownership, understanding the LLCs in detail is important for promoting asset preservation and getting the most out of your business.

In this book, we'll dive deeper into the basic ideas behind LLCs and discuss why they have indeed superseded other popular business structures. By their flexible management structure as well as the unmatched protection that they provide to the business owners, LLCs are one of the most versatile and advantageous business entities available.

However, if you are looking for an option, why choose the LLC form over others? We'll go into further detail in relation to the main benefits of LLCs that include asset protection, tax optimization and minimization as well as easy management. After you have finished reading this book, you will know why an LLC is the best option for your business.

Here's a brief overview of what's covered in "Crafting Your Perfect LLC":

Understanding the Concept of Limited Liability Companies: We will first analyze the main parts of LLCs, namely their formation, governance, and legal protection. After that, you will know why LLCs are generally chosen by first time businessmen and the differences between them and other business forms.

Why Choose an LLC Structure?: In this section, we will study the numerous advantages of forming an LLC, such as restricting the liability of owners personal assets from business liabilities and pass-through taxation. You will be able to make a wise decision about the structure of your business by learning the benefits that an LLC provides.

Overview of What's Covered: We will provide a roadmap to the topics that will be presented throughout the book so that you will know the valuable insights and practical tips you will have an opportunity to gain at the end of reading.

For those who are just beginning their entrepreneurial adventure or are looking to restructure their business, "Crafting Your Perfect LLC" is the perfect guide for understanding the complexities of Limited Liability Companies. Let's set off on this trip jointly and discover the great opportunities your business conceals.

Chapter 1
Setting the Foundation

Setting Foundation is like building a solid base for your business, establishing a strong foundation is similar to creating a stable ground. It is just about creating a platform for your business to take roots which is the first step to cultivating a successful business. From clarifying your business goals and values to framing relevant processes and structures, you stand a better chance when considering each step in the beginning as it sets the tone of your business situation. Imagine it as the foundation of a house without a solid base, the entire house will be shaky. Hence, make sure that you set a solid foundation for your business by noting down everything important at the beginning.

1.1 Evaluating Your Business Idea.

Evaluating your business idea is like taking a close look at your business from all sides, so you can tell if it's worth pursuing. It feels like you are delivering your idea to the product examination table so it can prove its world-readiness.

Firstly, you should ask yourself some important questions. Does your product or service have a market? What are the best segments of customer for your business; how many potential customers are there? Can your idea produce sufficient money to not just fund your business, but also to pay your bills and cover your personal expenses?

One of the ways to figure out whether your product or service is in demand is by doing some research. To stay ahead of the curve, look at how similar businesses are doing. Are they successful? If so, why? When not, you need to pinpoint the problem. Not only that but you can also talk to people who might be interested in your idea and ask for their opinions. Is it their opinion that this should come into existence or not? Will they see it worth it to spend money for it?

Another aspect to look into is your competition. What are the competitors out there and their offerings? In this event, be sure to express your uniqueness. What is the factor that will make customers choose you from the rest of them? You would have a USP which is a unique selling proposition. It separates you from the rest and makes you feel unique as well. Then consider your market segment. Who will buy your product or service? What do they like? What do they need? What actually are they ready to pay for? The more decent understanding of your customers you have, the more chances you have to fulfill their requirements and make them satisfied.

You'll also have to consider how you'll get the money from your business. Will you sell products? Offer services? Charge a subscription fee? You definitely need to calculate your pricing strategy and ensure you are offered competitive prices. Besides, you need to visualize funds and consider the time it will take to become self-sufficient.

Lastly, make sure your business plan is realistic. Do you have the capabilities to give an extra push if you are deprived of the skills and resources which you need to be successful? Do you feel the time factor would affect your business plan? Is the cash flow sufficient to implement the idea? Do you have a strategy for how you are going to expand your business over time? After answering all these questions you will find out whether your business plan is "actionable" and whether it can be successful. If it does, good luck with that, unless you did not know you were closer to making your fantasy come true. In the case that you are not satisfied with your current job, don't give up. Empower yourself by the education you've gained and endeavor to generate an improved version. Dedication and perseverance are key to achieving notable success in the business arena, allowing you to materialize your entrepreneurial dreams in no time.

1.2 Assessing Feasibility and Viability.

Assessing feasibility and viability is crucial when starting or expanding a business. It involves carefully analyzing if a business idea is practical and if it can succeed in the market.

Feasibility means asking if something is possible. In business, it's about determining if your idea can be done within your resources, like money, time, and skills. For example, if you want to start a bakery but lack baking experience, it might not be feasible unless you learn or hire someone who can bake.

Viability, on the other hand, is about whether your idea can sustain itself and make a profit in the long run. Even if something is possible, it might not be viable if it can't make money or cover its costs. For instance, if you plan to sell handmade sweaters in a hot climate where people rarely need sweaters, it might not be a viable business.

To assess feasibility and viability, you need to conduct thorough research, this includes having the right information about your competitors, understanding your target market, and industry trends. You'll want to know if there's demand for your product or service, who your potential customers are, and how much they're willing to pay. Financial feasibility is a big part of the assessment. You'll need to estimate your startup costs, ongoing expenses, and potential revenue. This helps you determine if you can afford to start and run the business, and if it can generate enough profit to sustain itself.

Market research is essential for understanding your target customers and competition. You can gather data through surveys, interviews, or analyzing existing market reports. This helps you tailor your product or service to meet the needs of your customers and differentiate yourself from competitors. Also, considering the legal and regulatory environment is important. You need to ensure that your business complies with all laws and regulations, such as permits, licenses, and taxes. Ignoring these requirements can lead to fines or even the closure of your business.

Technology and infrastructure are also important factors. You'll need to assess if you have access to the necessary tools, equipment, and facilities to operate your business efficiently. For example, if you're starting an online store, you'll need a reliable internet connection and a user-friendly website. Risk assessment is crucial too. Every business venture comes with risks, such as market changes, competition, or unexpected expenses. By identifying potential risks upfront, you can develop strategies to mitigate them and increase your chances of success.

1.3 Defining Your Mission and Vision.

Defining your mission and vision is crucial for any business. It's like setting the compass for your journey. Your mission is what your business does every day, why it exists. It's the heartbeat of your company, driving its actions and decisions. Your vision is where you want to be in the future, what you aspire to achieve. Together, they guide your business towards success.

Let's start with the mission. It's about your purpose, your reason for being. When defining your mission, ask yourself: What do we do? Who do we do it for? How do we do it? Your mission should be clear, concise, and inspiring. It should capture the essence of your business and resonate with your stakeholders, customers, employees, investors, and the community. No For example, a mission statement for a coffee shop could be: "To provide our customers with the finest quality coffee in a cozy and welcoming environment, while fostering community connections and sustainable practices."

Let's talk about vision. Your vision is your destination, your long-term goal. It's what motivates and excites you and your team. When crafting your vision, think big and bold. Imagine where you want your business to be in five, ten, or twenty years. What impact do you want to make? How do you envision the future of your industry? Continuing with the coffee shop example, a vision statement could be: "To become the preferred destination for coffee enthusiasts, known for our artisanal blends, warm hospitality, and commitment to environmental stewardship. We envision a world where every cup supports sustainable coffee farming and vibrant local communities."

Your mission and vision should complement each other, working together to inspire and guide your business. They should be authentic and aligned with your values. Your mission is your present, what you do every day to fulfill your purpose. Your vision is your future, the destination you're striving to reach. Both are essential for creating a roadmap for success and rallying your team around a shared purpose.

Once you've defined your mission and vision, it's important to communicate them effectively. Communicate your vision and mission with your team, customers, and stakeholders. Make them part of your company culture and decision-making processes. And remember, your mission and vision aren't set in stone. As your business evolves, you may need to revisit and refine them. But by defining them early on, you'll have a solid foundation to build upon and a clear direction to follow on your journey towards success.

Chapter 2
Legal Framework

The legal framework for business is like the rules of the game. It sets out the laws and regulations that companies need to follow. This includes things like contracts, intellectual property rights, taxes, and employment laws. Basically, it's all about making sure everyone plays fair and stays within the boundaries set by the law.

2.1 The Basics of Business Law and Regulations.

Business law and regulations are like the rules for businesses. They torchlight the do's and don't in businesses. Here are some basic things about business law:

Contracts: Contracts are agreements between people or companies. They say what each side has to do. For example, if you buy something from a store, you have a contract with them.

Employment Law: This is about how workers and bosses should treat each other.

It talks about pay, hours, and how safe the workplace should be.

Intellectual Property: This is about protecting ideas and creations. It includes things like patents for inventions, copyrights for books or music, and trademarks for logos.

Regulations: Governments make rules for businesses to follow. These rules cover things like safety, the environment, and how businesses can sell their products.

Understanding these basics helps businesses run smoothly and stay out of trouble. If a business breaks these rules, they can get in trouble with the law. So, it's important for businesses to know and follow them.

2.2 Comparing Business Structures: LLCs vs. Other Entities.

When comparing business structures, one common choice is between forming a Limited Liability Company (LLC) and other entities like sole proprietorships, partnerships, and corporations. Let's break down the main differences:

LLC (Limited Liability Company)

Provides limited liability protection, meaning the owners personal assets are protected from business debts and liabilities. Offers flexibility in management and tax structure. Members can choose to be taxed as a sole proprietorship, partnership, S-corporation, or C-corporation.

Requires a low amount of paperwork and formalities when compared to corporations.

Other Entities

Sole Proprietorship: Simplest form of business structure where one person owns and operates the business. No legal distinction between the owner and the business, so the owner has unlimited personal liability for business debts.

Partnership: Similar to a sole proprietorship but involves two or more individuals sharing ownership and responsibilities. Partners share profits and losses, and each partner is personally liable for the partnership's debts.

Corporation: A legal entity owned by shareholders is known as a corporation. Provides limited liability protection to shareholders, but is subject to double taxation (taxed at both the corporate level and individual level on dividends). Corporations require more formalities and paperwork, such as regular shareholder meetings and annual reports.

Forming an LLC provides a balance of liability protection, flexibility, and simplicity compared to other business structures. However, the best choice depends on factors like the nature of the business, the number of owners, and tax considerations. Consulting with a legal or financial advisor can help make the right decision for your business.

2.3 Understanding Legal Liabilities and Protections.

Understanding legal liabilities and protections in business is crucial for staying out of trouble and safeguarding your interests. Legal liabilities refer to the responsibilities and obligations that businesses have under the law, while legal protections are measures that can shield businesses from certain risks and liabilities. One major legal liability for businesses is the risk of being sued. If a business fails to fulfill its obligations, breaches a contract, or harms someone, it can be sued for damages. This could result in financial losses, damage to reputation, or even closure of the business. To protect against lawsuits, businesses can take measures such as drafting clear contracts, providing quality products and services, and obtaining liability insurance. Another important aspect of legal liabilities is compliance with laws and regulations. Businesses must adhere to various laws related to taxation, employment, health and safety, environmental protection, and more. Failure to comply with these laws can result in fines, legal penalties, or even criminal charges. To mitigate these risks, businesses should stay informed about relevant laws and seek legal advice when needed.

Legal protections can help businesses minimize their liabilities and mitigate risks. One common protection is limited liability, which shields business owners from personal responsibility for the debts and obligations of the business. This means that if the business is sued or goes bankrupt, the personal assets of the owners are generally protected. Contracts also provide important legal protections for businesses. By clearly outlining the rights and responsibilities of each party, contracts help prevent misunderstandings and disputes. Additionally, including clauses such as indemnity and limitation of liability can further protect businesses from certain risks.

Understanding legal liabilities and protections is essential for running a successful and compliant business. By being aware of potential risks, taking proactive measures to minimize liabilities, and seeking legal advice when needed, businesses can protect themselves and thrive in a competitive marketplace.

Chapter 3

Forming Your LLC

Forming an LLC, or Limited Liability Company, is a way to legally structure a business. Also, legally structuring a business means setting it up in a way that follows the rules and regulations.

3.1 Step-by-Step Guide to LLC Formation.

1. Choose a Name: Pick a unique name for your LLC that complies with state regulations. It usually needs to include "LLC" or "Limited Liability Company" at the end.

2. File Articles of Organization: You'll need to file articles of organization with the state where you want to form your LLC. This document typically includes your LLC's name, address, purpose, and the name and address of a registered agent who will receive legal documents on behalf of the LLC.

3. Choose a Registered Agent: A registered agent is a person or company designated to

receive legal documents and official notices on behalf of the LLC. This agent must have a physical address in the state where the LLC is formed.

4. Create an Operating Agreement: While not always required by law, it's a good idea to create an operating agreement. In this document the ownership and operating procedures of the LLC has been outlined. It can help prevent misunderstandings among LLC members and protect the company's limited liability status.

5. Obtain Licenses and Permits: Depending on your business type and location, you may need to obtain business licenses or permits from federal, state, or local government agencies. Research what's required for your specific business.

6. File Annual Reports: Some states require LLCs to file annual reports and pay a fee to keep the LLC in good standing. Make sure to stay updated on these requirements to avoid penalties or dissolution of the LLC.

7. Get an Employer Identification Number (EIN): An EIN is a unique nine-digit

number assigned by the IRS to identify your business for tax purposes. You'll need an EIN if your LLC has more than one member, if you hire employees, or if you choose to be taxed as a corporation.

8. Open a Business Bank Account: Keep your personal and business finances separate by opening a bank account for your LLC. This helps maintain the limited liability protection and makes it easier to track business expenses and income.

Follow these steps to successfully form an LLC and enjoy the benefits of limited liability while operating your business.

3.2 Choosing the Right State for Registration.

Choosing the right state for registering your Limited Liability Company (LLC) is an important decision. Each state has its own laws and regulations that can affect your business.

One factor to consider is the cost of formation. Some states have lower filing fees and annual renewal fees for LLCs, which can save you money in the long run. Additionally, some states offer tax incentives or breaks for businesses, so it's worth researching the tax rates and regulations in different states. Another consideration is the ease of doing business. Some states have simpler and faster registration processes for LLCs, while others may have more paperwork or requirements. You'll want to choose a state where the registration process is straightforward and efficient.

Legal protections are also important to consider. Some states offer stronger legal protections for LLC owners, such as better liability protection or clearer rules for business disputes. It's important to choose a state where your business interests are well-protected under the law. Lastly, you'll want to think about where your business will primarily operate. While you can register your LLC in any state, you may need to qualify to do business in other states if you have a physical presence or significant operations there. This can involve extra paperwork and fees, so it's often easier to register your LLC in the state where you do most of your business.

Overall, choosing the right state for registering your LLC involves considering factors like cost, ease of doing business, legal protections, and where your business operates. Researching your options and consulting with legal and financial professionals can help you make the best decision for your business.

3.3 Naming Your LLC: Tips and Considerations.

Naming your LLC is an important step in setting up your business. Below are some considerations and tips to keep in mind:

1. Relevance: Choose a name that reflects what your business does or sells. This helps customers to understand exactly what you have to offer.

2. Uniqueness: Make sure the name you choose is not already taken by another business in your state. You can search the availability of a name through your state's Secretary of State website.

3. Memorability: Pick a name that is easy to remember and spell. This makes it easier for customers to find you online and refer your business to others.

4. Avoiding Restricted Words: Some words, like "bank" or "insurance," may require special permissions or licenses to use in your business name. Make sure you understand any restrictions on certain words before choosing your name.

5. Legal Requirements: Your LLC name must include the abbreviation "LLC" or the full phrase "Limited Liability Company." This helps indicate to customers and partners that your business is structured as an LLC.

6. Trademark Check: Check if the name you want to use is already trademarked. You can search the United States Patent and Trademark Office (USPTO) database to see if the name is already in use.

7. Future Expansion: Consider whether the name will still be relevant if your business expands or diversifies its offerings in the future.

8. Online Availability: Check if the domain name for your business website is available. Having a matching domain name can help with branding and online visibility.

9. Feedback: Get feedback from friends, family, or potential customers on your chosen name. Feedbacks can help provide valuable insights and also help you make a final decision.

A proper consideration of these tips and factors can help you choose a name for your LLC that reflects your business's identity, is legally compliant, and resonates with your target audience.

Chapter 4
Crafting Your Operating Agreement.

Crafting an operating agreement is like making a rulebook for your business. It's a document that outlines how your company will be run and how decisions will be made. Even though it's not always required by law, having one can help avoid conflicts and protect your business. First, you need to decide what goes into your operating agreement. This can include things like how profits and losses will be divided, how decisions will be made, and what happens if someone wants to leave the business. Next, you'll want to write it down in clear and simple language that everyone involved can understand. It's important to be specific and cover as many scenarios as possible to avoid misunderstandings later on.

Once you've written your operating agreement, everyone involved in the business should review and sign it. This shows that everyone agrees to the rules laid out in the agreement. Then make sure to keep a copy of the operating agreement in a safe place where everyone can access it. You may need to refer to it in the future if any issues arise or if you need to make changes to the way your business operates. Crafting an operating agreement is an important step in setting up your business for success. It helps ensure that everyone is on the same page and can provide a framework for resolving disputes or making important decisions down the line.

4.1 Importance and Components of an Operating Agreement.

An operating agreement is like a rulebook for a business. It's important because it outlines how the business will be run and what happens if things don't go as planned.

One important component of an operating agreement is ownership. It specifies who owns the business and how much of it each owner has. This will help avoid disputes and confusion later on. Another important part is management. The operating agreement lays out who will make decisions for the business and how those decisions will be made. This helps keep things running smoothly and prevents disagreements about who is in charge. The agreement also addresses finances. It outlines how profits and losses will be divided among the owners and how the business will handle things like taxes and expenses. This helps ensure everyone knows what to expect financially. The operating agreement covers things like adding or removing owners, selling the business, and resolving disputes. These provisions help protect the interests of the owners and provide a roadmap for dealing with unexpected situations.

An operating agreement is crucial for clarifying the structure and operation of a business. It provides guidance for owners and helps prevent misunderstandings and conflicts down the road.

4.2 Customizing Your Agreement to Fit Your Business Needs.

Customizing your business agreement to fit your specific needs is crucial for protecting your interests and ensuring clarity in your business relationships. While there are many pre-made templates available, tailoring your agreement to address the unique aspects of your business can provide added security and prevent potential disputes down the line.

The first step in customizing your agreement is to identify the key terms and conditions that are relevant to your business. This may include pricing, payment terms, delivery schedules, and any specific obligations or responsibilities of each party involved. By clearly outlining these details in your agreement, you can minimize the risk of misunderstandings and ensure that both parties are on the same page. In addition to standard terms, you may also need to include provisions that address unique aspects of your business. For example, if you're providing services that require access to sensitive information or intellectual property, you'll want to include confidentiality and intellectual property protection clauses to safeguard your assets. Likewise, if your business involves the use of subcontractors or third-party vendors, you may need to outline their roles and responsibilities in the agreement to ensure smooth collaboration.

Another important consideration when customizing your agreement is to anticipate potential risks and liabilities and address them proactively. This may involve indemnification clauses to protect yourself against claims or damages arising from the actions of the other party, or limitation of liability clauses to cap your financial exposure in the event of a dispute. By clearly defining the scope of each party's liability, you can minimize the risk of costly litigation and ensure that both parties are adequately protected. Flexibility is also key when customizing your agreement. As your business grows and evolves, you may need to modify your agreement to accommodate changes in your operations or business model. By including provisions that allow for amendments or revisions to the agreement, you can adapt to changing circumstances without having to renegotiate the entire contract.

Communication is essential throughout the customization process. Make sure to discuss your needs and expectations with the other party involved and be open to their input and feedback. By fostering open and honest communication, you can ensure that both parties are fully satisfied with the terms of the agreement and minimize the risk of misunderstandings or disputes. Once you've customized your agreement, it's important to review it carefully to ensure that all the terms are clear, consistent, and legally enforceable. Consider seeking legal advice to review the agreement and ensure that it complies with relevant laws and regulations. Additionally, make sure to keep a signed copy of the agreement on file for your records and provide copies to all parties involved.

4.3 Common Mistakes to Avoid.

One common mistake is not customizing the operating agreement to fit the specific needs of the LLC. Each LLC is unique, and the operating agreement should reflect the goals and requirements of the business. Using a generic template without considering the specific circumstances of the company can lead to confusion and disputes among members.

Another mistake is not clearly defining the roles and responsibilities of each member. The operating agreement should outline the duties of each member, including their decision-making authority and management responsibilities. Failing to clearly define these roles can lead to disagreements and conflicts over who has the power to make important decisions for the company. It is also important to address how major decisions will be made within the LLC. This includes decisions such as admitting new members, taking on debt, or selling the company. Without a clear process for making these decisions, the LLC may struggle to move forward and make progress.

Failure to plan for the future is another common mistake. The operating agreement should include provisions for how the company will handle events such as the death or departure of a member, or the dissolution of the LLC. Without these provisions in place, the company may be left vulnerable to unexpected events that could threaten its stability. It's important to regularly review and update the operating agreement as the business grows and changes. Circumstances may evolve over time, and the operating agreement should reflect these changes to ensure that the company continues to operate smoothly and effectively. By avoiding these common mistakes and carefully crafting an operating agreement that meets the needs of the LLC, business owners can help set their company up for success.

Chapter 5:
Tax Matters

Understanding tax matters is crucial for any business owner to ensure compliance with the law and optimize financial performance. There are several key aspects of taxes that businesses need to consider:

Business Structure: The type of business structure chosen (sole proprietorship, partnership, corporation, or LLC) affects how the business is taxed. Each structure has different tax implications, including income tax, self-employment tax, and payroll taxes.

Tax Reporting: Businesses must report their income and expenses to the government accurately and on time. This typically involves filing various tax forms, such as the IRS Form 1040 for individuals or Form 1120 for corporations. Keeping thorough and organized financial records is essential for tax reporting.

Tax Deductions: Businesses can deduct certain expenses from their taxable income to reduce their tax liability. Common deductions include operating expenses, employee wages, rent, utilities, and depreciation of assets. Taking advantage of available deductions can lower the amount of taxes owed by the business.

Sales Tax: Depending on the nature of the business and its location, it may be required to collect and remit sales tax on goods or services sold to customers. Understanding the sales tax laws in the relevant jurisdictions is essential to avoid penalties for non-compliance.

Employment Taxes: Businesses that have employees are responsible for withholding and paying various employment taxes, including Social Security and Medicare taxes, federal and state income tax withholding, and unemployment taxes. Failing to properly withhold and pay these taxes can result in significant penalties.

Tax Planning: Strategic tax planning can help businesses minimize their tax burden and maximize their after-tax profits. This may involve timing income and expenses, taking advantage of tax credits and incentives, and structuring transactions in a tax-efficient manner.

Compliance: Staying compliant with tax laws and regulations is essential to avoid fines, penalties, and legal issues. Businesses should stay informed about changes to tax laws and seek professional advice when needed to ensure compliance.

Understanding the effective management of tax matters, businesses can maintain financial health, minimize risk, and maximize profitability. Consulting with a tax professional or accountant can provide valuable guidance and support in navigating the complexities of business taxes.

5.1 Tax Implications of LLCs.

It is important to understand the tax implications of forming an LLC. By default, the IRS treats LLCs as "pass-through" entities for tax purposes. This means that the profits and losses of the business are passed through to the owners, who report them on their personal tax returns. This can simplify tax filing because the LLC itself does not pay taxes directly. Instead, each owner pays taxes based on their share of the company's profits. However, LLC owners can choose how they want their business to be taxed, it is optional. They can elect to be taxed as a corporation instead of a pass-through entity. This decision can have significant implications for the business's tax liability.

If an LLC chooses to be taxed as a corporation, it will be subject to corporate income tax on its profits. Additionally, if the corporation distributes dividends to its owners, those dividends may be subject to individual income tax. This is known as "double taxation" because the profits are taxed at both the corporate and individual levels. Another important consideration for LLCs is self-employment tax. LLC owners who are actively involved in the day-to-day operations of the business may be subject to self-employment tax on their share of the company's profits. This tax helps fund Social Security and Medicare and is calculated based on the owner's share of the business's income.

To ensure compliance with tax laws and minimize tax liability, it's important for LLC owners to consult with a qualified tax professional. They can help determine the best tax structure for the business and provide guidance on tax planning strategies. By understanding the tax implications of forming an LLC, business owners can make informed decisions that benefit their bottom line.

5.2 Understanding Pass-through Taxation.

Understanding pass-through taxation is important for business owners, especially those with a sole proprietorship, partnership, or limited liability company (LLC). Pass-through taxation is a method of taxing business income where the profits "pass through" the business entity and are taxed at the individual level rather than at the entity level. When it comes to sole proprietorship, the business and the owner are considered the same entity for tax purposes. This means that all profits and losses from the business are reported on the owner's personal tax return. The owner pays income taxes on the business profits at their individual tax rate. Similarly, in a partnership, the business itself does not pay taxes on its income. Instead, the profits and losses "pass through" to the individual partners, who report their share of the income on their personal tax returns. Each partner is responsible for paying taxes on their share of the partnership income at their individual tax rate.

Limited liability companies (LLCs) also use pass-through taxation by default. Like partnerships, the income of an LLC passes through to its members, who report their share of the income on their personal tax returns. However, LLCs have the option to elect to be taxed as a corporation if they choose. There are several advantages to pass-through taxation. One benefit is that it simplifies the tax process for business owners. Instead of dealing with separate business tax returns, owners report their business income and deductions on their personal tax return, streamlining the process.

Pass-through taxation also allows business owners to take advantage of certain tax deductions and credits that may not be available to corporations. For example, self-employed individuals may be eligible to deduct expenses such as home office expenses, health insurance premiums, and retirement contributions.

However, there are also some limitations and considerations to keep in mind with pass-through taxation. One potential downside is that business owners may be subject to self-employment taxes, which cover Social Security and Medicare contributions. Additionally, pass-through entities may not be eligible for certain tax benefits available to corporations, such as lower tax rates on qualified dividends. Understanding pass-through taxation is crucial for business owners to effectively manage their tax obligations and maximize their tax benefits. By knowing how pass-through taxation works and consulting with tax professionals when needed, business owners can ensure that they are making informed decisions about their tax strategy.

5.3 Strategies for Tax Optimization.

Tax optimization is the process of legally reducing the amount of taxes a person or business owes. By implementing effective strategies, individuals and businesses can minimize their tax burden and keep more of their hard-earned money. Here are some simple strategies for tax optimization:

Maximize deductions and credits: Deductions and credits can help reduce taxable income and the amount of tax owed. Individuals should take advantage of deductions such as mortgage interest, charitable contributions, and medical expenses. For businesses, common deductions include expenses related to operating the business, such as rent, utilities, and employee salaries. Additionally, businesses may qualify for various tax credits, such as the research and development tax credit or the small business health care tax credit, which can further reduce their tax liability.

Contribute to retirement accounts: Contributing to retirement accounts, such as 401(k)s or IRAs, can provide immediate tax benefits. Contributions to these accounts are often tax-deductible, meaning they reduce taxable income for the year in which they are made. Additionally, earnings in these accounts grow tax-deferred until withdrawal, allowing individuals to potentially save even more on taxes in the long run.

Utilize tax-advantaged investment accounts: Investing in tax-advantaged accounts, such as Health Savings Accounts (HSAs) or 529 college savings plans, can offer tax benefits. Contributions to HSAs are tax-deductible, and withdrawals for qualified medical expenses are tax-free. Similarly, earnings in 529 plans grow tax-free and withdrawals for qualified education expenses are also tax-free.

Manage capital gains and losses: Selling investments strategically can help minimize capital gains taxes. By holding investments for more than a year, individuals qualify for lower long-term capital gains tax rates. Additionally, offsetting capital gains with capital losses can help reduce taxable income. Tax-loss harvesting, which involves selling investments at a loss to offset capital gains, can be a useful strategy for minimizing taxes.

Stay informed about tax law changes: Tax laws are subject to change, and staying informed about updates and revisions can help individuals and businesses adapt their tax planning strategies accordingly. Working with a knowledgeable tax professional can also provide valuable guidance and ensure compliance with current tax laws.

Overall, tax optimization requires careful planning and consideration of various factors. By implementing these strategies and staying proactive about managing taxes, individuals and businesses can maximize their tax savings and keep more of their money working for them.

Chapter 6:
Managing Your LLC

Managing your business is important for its success. There are several key aspects to consider when it comes to managing your company effectively. First, it's important to have a clear organizational structure. This includes defining the roles and responsibilities of each member of the team. By clearly outlining who is responsible for what, you can ensure that tasks are completed efficiently and that everyone is working towards the same goals.

Communication is also crucial for effective management. Regular communication with your team helps keep everyone informed about the company's progress, goals, and any changes that may occur. This will help prevent confusion or misunderstanding and ensure that everyone is on the same page.

Setting goals and objectives is another important part of managing your business. By setting specific, measurable goals, you can track your progress and stay focused on what needs to be done to achieve success. Regularly reviewing and updating your goals can help keep your business moving forward.

Financial management is essential for the health of your business. This includes keeping accurate records of your income and expenses, as well as budgeting and planning for the future. By staying on top of your finances, you can make informed decisions about how to allocate resources and grow your business.

Compliance with laws and regulations is also important for managing your business. This includes following tax laws, licensing requirements, and any other regulations that apply to your industry. Failing to comply with these laws can result in fines, legal trouble, and damage to your reputation. It's important to regularly evaluate and adjust your management strategies as needed. Business environments changes almost everyday and what works today may not work tomorrow. By staying flexible and open to change, you can adapt to new challenges and opportunities as they arise.

6.1 Roles and Responsibilities of LLC Members.

In a business, each member plays a specific role and has certain responsibilities to ensure the smooth operation of the company. Understanding these roles and responsibilities is crucial for the success of the business.

One important role within a business is that of the owner or member. Members are the individuals who have ownership interests in the company. Their primary responsibility is to contribute capital or assets to the business and share in the profits and losses according to their ownership stakes. Another key role within the business is that of the manager. It's the responsibility of a manager to oversee the day-to-day operations of the company. They make decisions about things like hiring and firing employees, managing finances, and setting goals and objectives for the business. Managers may be members of the company or they may be hired from outside the organization.

Members have a responsibility to participate in the management of the company. This may involve attending meetings, voting on important decisions, and providing input and guidance to the managers. Even if members are not directly involved in the day-to-day operations of the business, they still have a duty to ensure that the company is being run effectively and in accordance with its goals and objectives. One of the responsibilities of the members is to act in the best interests of the company. This means making decisions that are in line with the company's goals and objectives and avoiding conflicts of interest. Members should always act honestly and ethically and disclose any potential conflicts of interest to the other members. In addition to their management and decision-making responsibilities, members also have financial responsibilities to the company. This may include contributing capital to the business, repaying loans or debts owed to the company, and ensuring that the company's finances are managed responsibly.

Lastly, members have a duty to the other members of the company. This means communicating openly and honestly with each other, resolving conflicts in a constructive manner, and working together to achieve the company's goals.

6.2 Effective Communication and Decision-Making.

Effective communication and decision-making are crucial for the success of a limited liability company (LLC). In a small business setting, clear communication and sound decision-making processes help ensure that everyone is on the same page and working towards common goals.

Communication within an LLC should be open, honest, and transparent. This means sharing information freely among members and keeping everyone informed about important developments or decisions. Regular meetings, whether in person or virtual, provide opportunities for members to discuss progress, address concerns, and brainstorm ideas together. Active listening is one of the essential components of effective communication. Members should listen attentively to each other's perspectives and ideas, without interrupting or dismissing them. This fosters a culture of respect and collaboration within the LLC, where everyone feels valued and heard.

In addition to verbal communication, written communication is also important for documenting decisions and agreements. This includes keeping detailed records of meetings, decisions, and any changes to the operating agreement. Written communication helps prevent misunderstandings and provides a reference point for future discussions.

When it comes to decision-making in an LLC, it's important to involve all members in the process. Each member brings unique insights and expertise to the table, and their input can help ensure that decisions are well-informed and thoughtfully considered. Decisions should be made democratically, with each member having an equal voice and vote. Consensus-building is often the goal when making decisions within an LLC. This means working together to find solutions that everyone can agree on, rather than imposing decisions unilaterally. Sometimes, reaching consensus may require compromise or creative problem-solving, but it helps build trust and cohesion among members.

However, not all decisions can be made by consensus, especially in larger LLCs or when time is of the essence. In these cases, it may be necessary to designate certain individuals or committees to make decisions on behalf of the company. This delegation of authority should be clearly defined in the operating agreement and based on the expertise and experience of the individuals involved.

Regardless of how decisions are made, it's important to communicate them effectively to all members of the LLC. This includes explaining the rationale behind the decision, as well as any implications or next steps. Transparent communication helps ensure that everyone understands their role and responsibilities moving forward. By prioritizing effective communication and decision-making, LLCs can foster a positive and collaborative work environment where members feel empowered to contribute their ideas and expertise. This not only leads to better outcomes for the company but also strengthens relationships and morale among its members.

6.3 Handling Disputes and Challenges.

Handling disputes and challenges in a Limited Liability Company (LLC) is important to maintain harmony and keep the business running smoothly. Here are some simple strategies for addressing and resolving conflicts within an LLC.

Open Communication: Encourage open and honest communication among members. Establishing a culture where members feel comfortable discussing issues and concerns can help prevent conflicts from escalating. Regular meetings can provide opportunities for members to address any issues and work towards solutions together.

Establish Clear Procedures: Define clear procedures for making decisions and resolving disputes within the operating agreement. This document should outline how major decisions will be made, how conflicts will be addressed, and what steps will be taken to resolve disputes. Having these procedures in place can help prevent misunderstandings and disagreements from escalating into more serious conflicts.

Seek Mediation: When conflicts arise, consider seeking mediation to help resolve them. Mediation involves a neutral third party who can help facilitate communication and negotiation between those involved. Mediation can be a less formal and less expensive alternative to litigation, and it allows the parties to work together to find mutually agreeable solutions.

Consult Legal Counsel: In some cases, it may be necessary to seek legal advice to resolve disputes within an LLC. An attorney with experience in business law can provide guidance on how to navigate the legal aspects of the dispute and help protect the interests of the company and its members. Legal counsel can also help ensure that any resolutions reached are legally enforceable.

Focus on the Best Interests of the Company: Remind members to focus on what is best for the company as a whole, rather than individual interests. Encourage members to set aside personal differences and work towards common goals for the success of the business. Emphasizing the importance of collaboration and teamwork can help reduce conflicts and promote a positive working environment.

Document Everything: Keep thorough records of all decisions, agreements, and communications within the company. Having documentation of discussions and agreements can help prevent misunderstandings and provide clarity in the event of a dispute. It also serves as a valuable reference point for resolving conflicts and ensuring that all parties are held accountable.

Review and Update the Operating Agreement: Regularly review and update the operating agreement to ensure that it accurately reflects the current needs and circumstances of the LLC. As the business grows and changes, certain provisions may need to be revised or added to address new challenges or opportunities. By keeping the operating agreement up-to-date, the LLC can adapt more effectively to changes and reduce the likelihood of conflicts arising.

Chapter 7
Growing Your LLC

Growing your limited liability company (LLC) is an exciting journey that requires careful planning, dedication, and strategic decision-making. Whether you're just starting out or looking to expand an existing LLC, there are several key steps you can take to foster growth and success.

Set Clear Goals: Before you can effectively grow your LLC, it's important to establish clear and achievable goals. Determine what you want to accomplish with your business, whether it's increasing revenue, expanding into new markets, or launching new products or services. Having specific goals in mind will help guide your growth strategy and keep your efforts focused.

Know Your Market: Understanding your target market is essential for growing your LLC. Conduct market research to identify your ideal customers, their needs, and preferences. By gaining insights into your market, you can tailor your products or services to better meet customer demands and differentiate yourself from competitors.

Focus on Customer Satisfaction: Satisfied customers are more likely to become repeat customers and recommend your business to others. Make customer satisfaction a priority by providing excellent products or services, delivering exceptional customer service, and soliciting feedback to continually improve your offerings.

Build a Strong Online Presence: In today's digital age, having a strong online presence is crucial for growing your LLC. Create a professional website to showcase your products or services and provide valuable information to potential customers. Utilize social media platforms to engage with your audience, share updates, and build brand awareness. Invest in search engine optimization (SEO) to improve your website's visibility and attract more organic traffic.

Invest in Marketing: Effective marketing is essential for attracting new customers and promoting your LLC's growth. Develop a comprehensive marketing strategy that utilizes a mix of online and offline tactics, such as social media marketing, email marketing, content marketing, and traditional advertising. Allocate resources wisely to maximize the impact of your marketing efforts and reach your target audience effectively.

Expand Your Offerings: Diversifying your product or service offerings can help attract new customers and increase revenue streams. Consider expanding your product line or introducing complementary services that align with your existing offerings and appeal to your target market. Be sure to conduct thorough market research and assess demand before launching new products or services.

Form Strategic Partnerships: Collaborating with other businesses or organizations can provide valuable opportunities for growth. Look for potential partners who complement your offerings or target the same audience. Forming strategic partnerships can help expand your reach, increase brand exposure, and open doors to new opportunities for collaboration and growth.

Focus on Efficiency and Productivity: Streamlining your operations and maximizing efficiency is key to scaling your LLC effectively. Identify areas where you can automate processes, eliminate unnecessary tasks, and improve workflow efficiency. Invest in technology and tools that can help streamline operations, boost productivity, and free up time for strategic initiatives.

Invest in Talent: Surrounding yourself with talented and dedicated employees is essential for growing your LLC. Hire skilled professionals who share your vision and are committed to helping your business succeed. Invest in ongoing training and development to empower your team and enhance their skills and capabilities.

Stay Flexible and Adapt to Change: The business landscape is constantly evolving, and it's important to stay flexible and adapt to changing market conditions and customer preferences. Be open to new ideas, embrace innovation, and be willing to pivot your strategy as needed to capitalize on emerging opportunities and overcome challenges.

Monitor Financial Performance: Keep a close eye on your LLC's financial performance to ensure sustainable growth and profitability. Regularly monitor key financial metrics, such as revenue, expenses, cash flow, and profitability. Use this data to make informed decisions, identify areas for improvement, and adjust your strategy as needed to achieve your financial goals.

Seek Professional Advice: Growing your LLC can be a complex and challenging process, and seeking professional advice can provide valuable guidance and support along the way. Consider working with business consultants, financial advisors, or legal experts who can offer insights, expertise, and strategic advice to help you navigate the challenges of growth and position your LLC for success.

By following these tips and staying focused on your goals, you can effectively grow your LLC and achieve long-term success in the competitive business landscape. Remember to be patient, persistent, and proactive in pursuing growth opportunities, and don't hesitate to seek help and advice when needed. With dedication, hard work, and strategic planning, you can take your LLC to new heights and realize its full potential.

7.1 Scaling Strategies and Expansion Plans.

Scaling strategies and expansion plans are essential for growing businesses. Scaling means increasing the size and scope of a business to accommodate more customers, generate higher revenue, and ultimately achieve greater success. Expansion refers to the specific actions taken to grow the business, whether it's entering new markets, adding new products or services, or increasing operational capacity. Here, we'll explore various scaling strategies and expansion plans in simple terms.

1. Market Penetration:
Market penetration involves selling more of your existing products or services to your current customer base or reaching new customers within your current market. This strategy focuses on increasing market share by offering promotions, discounts, or improving marketing efforts to attract more customers. For example, a coffee shop might offer a loyalty program to encourage repeat

business and attract new customers by advertising in local newspapers or on social media.

2. Product Development:
Product development involves creating new products or improving existing ones to meet the changing needs or preferences of customers. This strategy allows businesses to expand their offerings and attract new customers while also retaining existing ones. For example, a tech company might release a new version of its software with additional features based on customer feedback or market trends.

3. Market Development:
Market development involves entering new markets or expanding into different geographical areas to reach new customers. This strategy allows businesses to tap into new customer segments or regions where there is demand for their products or services. For example, a clothing retailer might expand into international markets by opening stores in other countries or selling its products online to customers around the world.

4. Diversification:
Diversification involves expanding into new markets or industries that are unrelated to your current business activities. This strategy helps businesses spread risk and take advantage of new opportunities for growth. For example, a food company might diversify its product line by introducing a new line of beverages or snacks, or it might enter into the hospitality industry by opening a chain of restaurants.

5. Franchising:
Franchising involves licensing your business model and brand to third-party operators, known as franchisees, who run their own locations. This strategy allows businesses to rapidly expand their presence without incurring the costs and risks associated with opening new locations themselves. For example, a fast-food restaurant might franchise its brand to individuals who want to open their own restaurants in different cities or countries.

6. Joint Ventures and Partnerships:
Joint ventures and partnerships involve collaborating with other businesses to achieve mutual goals, such as entering new

markets or developing new products. This strategy allows businesses to leverage the resources, expertise, and networks of their partners to accelerate growth. For example, a technology company might form a partnership with a manufacturing company to develop and produce a new product together.

7. Acquisitions:
Acquisitions involve purchasing other businesses to expand your own operations or enter new markets quickly. This strategy allows businesses to gain access to new customers, technologies, or resources without having to build them from scratch. For example, a retail company might acquire a competitor to increase its market share or acquire a technology startup to access its innovative products or talent.

8. Vertical Integration:
Vertical integration involves expanding into different stages of the supply chain, either backward towards suppliers or forward towards customers. This strategy allows businesses to control more aspects of their operations and reduce costs while also improving efficiency and quality. For

example, a clothing manufacturer might acquire a textile factory to produce its own fabric or a retail chain might acquire a distribution company to streamline its logistics.

Scaling strategies and expansion plans are essential for growing businesses. Whether it's increasing market share, developing new products, entering new markets, or forming strategic partnerships, businesses have many options for scaling and expanding their operations. By carefully planning and implementing these strategies, businesses can achieve sustainable growth and long-term success.

7.2 Funding Options for LLC Growth.

Funding options for LLC growth vary depending on the stage of the business and its specific needs. Here are some common funding options that LLCs can consider:

Bootstrapping: Bootstrapping means using personal savings or revenue generated by the business to fund its growth. This is often the first option for many small LLCs, as it allows them to retain full control and ownership of the company. While bootstrapping may limit the speed of growth, it can also be a cost-effective way to build the business without taking on debt or giving up equity.

Friends and Family: Some LLCs may turn to friends and family members for funding. This can involve borrowing money from loved ones or inviting them to invest in the business in exchange for ownership stake. While borrowing from friends and family can be a relatively easy and low-cost way to raise capital, it's important to clearly outline the terms of the agreement and consider the potential impact on personal relationships.

Small Business Administration (SBA) Loans: The Small Business Administration offers several loan programs designed to help small businesses, including LLCs, access funding. These loans typically have lower interest rates and longer repayment terms than traditional bank loans, making them an attractive option for businesses looking to finance growth initiatives such as expanding operations or purchasing equipment.

Bank Loans: Traditional bank loans are another option for LLCs seeking funding. Banks may offer term loans, lines of credit, or other financing options tailored to the needs of small businesses. While bank loans can provide access to larger amounts of capital, they may also require a strong credit history and collateral to secure the loan.

Venture Capital: Venture capital firms invest in early-stage companies with high growth potential in exchange for equity ownership. While venture capital can provide significant funding to fuel rapid growth, it often comes with strict terms and conditions, as well as giving up a portion of ownership and control of the business.

Angel Investors: Angel investors are individuals who provide funding to startups and small businesses in exchange for ownership equity. Like venture capital firms, angel investors can offer substantial capital and expertise to help LLCs grow. However, they may also expect a high return on their investment and may require a significant ownership stake in the company.

Crowdfunding: Crowdfunding platforms allow businesses to raise funds from a large number of individuals, typically through online campaigns. This can be a viable option for LLCs seeking to raise capital for specific projects or product launches. Crowdfunding can also help generate buzz and awareness for the business among potential customers and investors.

Grants and Government Programs: Some LLCs may be eligible for grants or funding from government agencies or nonprofit organizations. These programs often focus on specific industries or regions and may require meeting certain criteria or objectives. While grants can provide valuable funding without the need for repayment, they may also be competitive and time-consuming to secure.

It's important for LLCs to carefully consider their funding options and choose the approach that best aligns with their growth goals, financial situation, and risk tolerance. By exploring multiple funding sources and weighing the pros and cons of each, LLCs can position themselves for sustainable growth and success.

7.3 Building a Strong Brand and Reputation.

Building a strong brand and reputation is essential for any business. A strong brand and reputation can help a business stand out from the competition, attract customers, and foster loyalty. Here are some key steps to building a strong brand and reputation:

Define Your Brand: The first step in building a strong brand is to clearly define what your business stands for. This includes identifying your target audience, your unique selling proposition (what sets you apart from competitors), and your brand values. Your brand should reflect the personality of your business and resonate with your target customers.

Consistent Branding: Consistency is key when it comes to building a strong brand. Your brand should be consistent across all touchpoints, including your logo, website, social media profiles, marketing materials, and customer interactions. Consistent branding helps to reinforce your brand identity and build trust with customers.

Deliver Exceptional Customer Experience: Building a strong reputation starts with delivering exceptional customer experiences. From the moment a customer interacts with your business to after-sales support, every interaction should be positive and memorable. Providing excellent customer service and exceeding expectations can help build trust and loyalty with customers.

Be Authentic: Authenticity is important when building a strong brand and reputation. Be true to your brand values and mission, and avoid trying to be something you're not. Authentic brands are more relatable and trustworthy, which can help build stronger connections with customers.

Engage with Your Audience: Building a strong brand requires active engagement with your audience. Use social media, email marketing, and other channels to engage with your customers, gather feedback, and respond to their needs. Building a community around your brand can help strengthen loyalty and advocacy.

Build Partnerships and Collaborations: Collaborating with other businesses or influencers can help expand your reach and build credibility for your brand. Look for opportunities to partner with like-minded businesses or influencers that align with your brand values and target audience.

Monitor and Manage Your Reputation: Your brand's reputation is crucial to its success. Monitor online reviews, social media mentions, and other feedback channels to stay aware of what people are saying about your brand. Address any negative feedback or complaints immediately and professionally to protect your brand's name and reputation.

Stay Consistent with Your Messaging: Consistency in messaging is important for building a strong brand and reputation. Your brand messaging should correspond with your brand values and resonate with your target audience. Whether it's through advertising, social media, or customer communications, ensure that your messaging is clear, compelling, and consistent.

Deliver Quality Products and Services: Ultimately, the strength of your brand and reputation will depend on the quality of your products or services. Delivering high-quality products or services that meet or exceed customer expectations is essential for building trust and loyalty. Invest in product development, quality control, and customer feedback to continuously improve and innovate.

Chapter 8
Compliance and Maintenance

In a limited liability company (LLC), compliance and maintenance are important for keeping the business running smoothly and legally. Compliance simply means following the rules and regulations set by the federal government and other authorities. Maintenance involves regularly taking care of the administrative and legal aspects of the LLC. One key aspect of compliance is filing necessary paperwork with the government. This includes registering the LLC with the appropriate state authorities and obtaining any required licenses or permits to operate legally. Failure to comply with these requirements can result in fines, sanctions or even the closure of the business.

LLCs must also comply with tax laws. This includes filing annual tax returns and paying any taxes owed to the government. Additionally, LLCs may need to comply with specific industry regulations or laws that apply to their business activities. Maintenance of an LLC involves keeping accurate and up-to-date records. This includes maintaining financial records, such as accounting books and bank statements, as well as records of important company decisions, such as meeting minutes and resolutions. Keeping thorough records is not only important for compliance but also for protecting the members' limited liability protection. Regular meetings of the LLC's members or managers may also be required to make important decisions and keep the business running smoothly. These meetings should be documented in writing to ensure compliance with legal requirements.

Know that it is important for LLCs to stay informed about any changes in laws or regulations that may affect their business. This may involve consulting with legal or financial professionals to ensure ongoing compliance with all applicable laws and regulations. By prioritizing compliance and maintenance, LLCs can minimize the risk of legal issues and keep their businesses running smoothly and successfully.

8.1 Annual Requirements and Ongoing Obligations.

Annual requirements and ongoing obligations are important tasks that businesses need to complete regularly to maintain compliance with laws and regulations. These requirements ensure that businesses operate legally and smoothly. One common annual requirement is filing taxes. Businesses must file their tax returns every year, reporting their income and expenses to the government. This helps determine how much tax the business owes and ensures that it pays its fair share to fund public services.

Another ongoing obligation is keeping accurate financial records. Businesses need to track their income, expenses, and other financial transactions throughout the year. This not only helps with tax compliance but also provides valuable information for making business decisions and securing financing. Businesses also have ongoing obligations to their employees. This includes paying wages and benefits, providing a safe work environment, and complying with employment laws. By meeting these obligations, businesses can attract and retain talented employees and avoid legal issues.

Maintaining proper business licenses and permits is another ongoing obligation.

Depending on the type of business and its location, it may need various licenses and permits to operate legally. Renewing these licenses and permits on time ensures that the business can continue operating without interruption. Compliance with regulations is a continuous obligation for businesses. This includes regulations related to safety, environmental protection, consumer rights, and more. Staying informed about changes in regulations and making any necessary adjustments to business practices helps businesses avoid fines, lawsuits, and other penalties. Overall, annual requirements and ongoing obligations are essential for the smooth and legal operation of businesses. By staying on top of these tasks, businesses can maintain compliance, protect their interests, and contribute to their long-term success.

8.2 Staying Compliant with State and Federal Regulations.

Staying compliant with state and federal regulations means following the rules set by the government to run a business legally. These regulations cover many areas, including taxes, employment, safety, and more. An important aspect of compliance is paying taxes. Businesses must accurately report their income and pay taxes to both the state and federal governments. Failure to do so can result in a serious penalty and fines.

Employment laws also require compliance. This includes paying employees fairly, providing a safe working environment, and following anti-discrimination laws. Violating these laws can lead to lawsuits and other legal consequences. Businesses must also comply with regulations specific to their industry. For example, food businesses must follow health and safety regulations, while financial institutions must adhere to banking laws.

To stay compliant, businesses should stay informed about changes in regulations and regularly review their practices to ensure they are following the law. Seeking legal advice when needed can help ensure compliance and avoid legal trouble. By staying compliant with state and federal regulations, businesses can operate legally, protect their employees and customers, and avoid costly penalties and fines.

8.3 Strategies for Long-Term Success.

Long-term success in a limited liability company (LLC) requires careful planning and strategic thinking. Here are some simple strategies to help ensure the long-term success of your LLC:

Set Clear Goals: Define your long-term objectives and create a roadmap for achieving them. Having clear goals will help guide your decisions and keep your business on track.

Build Strong Relationships: Cultivate positive relationships with customers, suppliers, and stakeholders. Good relationships can lead to repeat business, referrals, and opportunities for growth.

Focus on Quality: Deliver high-quality products or services consistently. Quality builds trust and loyalty among customers, which is essential for long-term success.

Adapt to Change: Stay flexible and adapt to changes in the market, technology, and industry regulations. Being able to pivot when necessary will help you stay relevant and competitive.

Invest in Your Team: Hire and retain talented employees who are committed to your company's success. Invest in training and development to help your team grow and thrive.

Manage Finances Wisely: Keep a close eye on your finances and manage cash flow effectively. Avoid unnecessary debt and keep expenses in check to ensure financial stability.

Innovate and Improve: Continuously look for ways to innovate and improve your products, services, and processes. Welcome new ideas and technologies to keep you ahead of the competition.

Protect Your Assets: Take steps to protect your intellectual property, assets, and brand reputation. This includes securing trademarks, patents, and copyrights, as well as implementing robust security measures.

Stay Compliant: Stay up-to-date with all legal and regulatory requirements.

Compliance with laws and regulations is essential for avoiding fines, lawsuits, and other costly consequences.

Monitor and Evaluate: Regularly monitor your performance against your goals and make adjustments as needed. Evaluate what's working well and what can be improved to ensure continued success.

By implementing these simple strategies and staying focused on your long-term goals, you can position your LLC for sustained success and growth.

Conclusion

In "Crafting Your Perfect LLC: From Concept to Creation," we've embarked on a journey from the initial spark of an idea to the establishment of a successful Limited Liability Company (LLC). Throughout this book, we've explored the essential steps, considerations, and strategies necessary to bring your vision to life in the form of a thriving business entity. As we reach the conclusion of our exploration, it's important to reflect on the key takeaways. Firstly, we've learned the importance of thorough planning and research in the early stages of forming an LLC. From selecting a suitable business name to understanding the legal requirements and tax implications, laying a solid foundation is crucial.

Furthermore, we've delved into the significance of crafting a comprehensive business plan that outlines your objectives, target market, competitive analysis, and financial projections. A well-defined plan serves as a roadmap, guiding your decisions and actions as you navigate the complexities of entrepreneurship. We've discussed the various options available for structuring your LLC, such as single-member vs. multi-member LLCs, and the implications of each choice on liability, management, and taxation. Understanding these nuances empowers you to make informed decisions aligned with your business goals. Additionally, we've emphasized the importance of compliance with state regulations and ongoing obligations, including annual filings, tax requirements, and record-keeping. Staying abreast of these responsibilities ensures the continued legality and success of your LLC.

In essence, "Crafting Your Perfect LLC: From Concept to Creation" serves as a comprehensive guide for aspiring entrepreneurs seeking to establish and grow their own LLCs. By following the insights and advice shared within these pages, you are equipped with the knowledge and tools necessary to navigate the journey of entrepreneurship with confidence and clarity. Remember, building a successful LLC is a journey, and with dedication, perseverance, and strategic planning, your dreams can become a reality.

Recap of Key Points

Here are some key points to always keep in mind from what you have read so far in this book about crafting a perfect LLC.

1. Research and Planning: Start by researching your business idea and market to ensure it's viable. Develop a solid business plan outlining your goals, target market, competition, and financial projections.

2. Choose a Name: Select a unique and memorable name for your LLC that reflects your brand identity. Ensure it complies with state regulations and is available for registration.

3. Registered Agent: Designate a registered agent who will receive legal documents and

official correspondence on behalf of your LLC.

4. File Articles of Organization: Prepare and file the Articles of Organization with the Secretary of State or relevant state agency. This document formally establishes your LLC and includes essential details such as the business name, address, registered agent, and management structure.

5. Operating Agreement: Draft an operating agreement that outlines the ownership structure, management responsibilities, decision-making processes, and distribution of profits and losses among members. While not always required by law, an operating agreement helps clarify expectations and minimize disputes.

6. Obtain Necessary Permits and Licenses: Research and obtain any required permits, licenses, or certifications necessary to operate your business legally. Requirements vary depending on the location and industry.

7. Tax ID Number: Apply for an Employer Identification Number (EIN) from the IRS. This unique identifier is necessary for tax

purposes, hiring employees, opening bank accounts, and more.

8. Open a Business Bank Account: Separate your business and personal finances by opening a dedicated business bank account. This helps maintain accurate records, simplifies tax filing, and protects personal assets.

9. Compliance and Ongoing Requirements: Stay compliant with ongoing requirements such as annual filings, taxes, and any state-specific obligations. Failure to comply could result in penalties or the loss of limited liability protection.

10. Protect Intellectual Property: Consider trademarking your business name, logo, or products to protect your brand identity and prevent others from using similar marks.

11. Insurance: Evaluate and obtain appropriate insurance coverage for your LLC, such as general liability insurance, property insurance, or professional liability insurance, depending on your industry and specific risks.

12. Build a Strong Team: As your business grows, hire qualified employees or contractors who align with your company culture and contribute to its success.

13. Marketing and Promotion: Develop a marketing strategy to promote your LLC and attract customers. Utilize online and offline channels such as social media, websites, networking events, and advertising to reach your target audience.

14. Adapt and Innovate: Stay adaptable and open to feedback, continuously seeking ways to improve your products or services and meet evolving customer needs. Regularly review and adjust your business strategies as necessary to remain competitive in the market.

Final Thoughts and Next Steps.

After going through the LLC guide book, it's important to summarize your final thoughts and plan your next steps in simple terms. Reflect on what you've learned and consider how it applies to your situation. Then, jot down your key takeaways and the actions you need to take next. This could include deciding whether forming an LLC is the right choice for your business, understanding the steps involved in the process, and outlining a timeline for implementation. Keep it clear and concise, focusing on actionable items to move forward effectively.